IMAGES
of America

NASELLE-GRAYS
RIVER VALLEY

ON THE COVER: Pictured is a 1913 hay-making party in Grays River, on the Frank Badger Farm. From left to right are George Sorenson, Frank Badger with son Harold in front of him, Ernest Strom, two unidentified, and Frank's son Arthur Badger. The man on top of the load is Clarence Worrell. (Appelo Archives.)

IMAGES
of America

NASELLE-GRAYS RIVER VALLEY

Donna Gatens-Klint and
the Appelo Archives

ARCADIA
PUBLISHING

Published by Arcadia Publishing
Charleston SC, Chicago IL, Portsmouth NH, San Francisco CA

Library of Congress Catalog Card Number: 2008934528

For all general information contact Arcadia Publishing at:
Telephone 843-853-2070
Fax 843-853-0044
E-mail sales@arcadiapublishing.com
For customer service and orders:
Toll-Free 1-888-313-2665

Visit us on the Internet at www.arcadiapublishing.com

This book is dedicated to Carlton Appelo, who has preserved the history of our area through pictures and written information.
It is also dedicated to the people of the area, whose pictures we have used to help make the Appelo Archives what it is today.

CONTENTS

ACKNOWLEDGMENTS

This book would not have been possible without the Appelo Archives and all the local people who have loaned pictures to the archives over the years. I especially want to thank Mike and Lisa Bighill, the Sorenson family, the Chadwick family, the Badger family, and the Brix family for all the pictures; my daughters, Janine Klint-Davis for helping me with the computer and Diane Klint-Brown for all her encouragement; and the staff at Appelo Archives—Maia Wise, Audrey Wirkkala, and Brandon Novoselic—for their help. I also want to thank Karen Bertroch and the Wahkiakum Community Foundation for giving me the opportunity to do this book. All images are courtesy of the Appelo Archives in Naselle, Washington.

INTRODUCTION

The Naselle-Grays River Valley and surrounding historical towns are located in western Wahkiakum County (the smallest county in the state of Washington) and the southern part of Pacific County. The Chinook Indians inhabited the area in the early years, and many of their descendants are still living here. It is also near the end of the Lewis and Clark Trail. In 1805, the famous explorers' expedition went the full length of Wahkiakum County along the mighty Columbia River.

All the old historical towns—like Brookfield, Dahlia, Altoona, Pillar Rock, Deep River, Oneida, Frankfort, Rosburg, and Knappton—which were only accessible by boat, are now just memories to be written about. Luckily there were many pictures taken, and now a lot of information has been recorded on many of these historical ghost towns.

In the late 1800s, Naselle was one of the smaller towns in the area. Today it is the largest and the only one that has survived, thanks to the many dedicated Finnish immigrant families that homesteaded the area, who still have many descendants living here. The original spelling for Naselle was Nasel. In 1921, it was changed to the current spelling.

Deep River, once one of the busiest early towns of our area, had many residents. The train and the logging camps were nearby. Deep River had several general stores, a restaurant, boardinghouse, hotel, barbershop, first aid clinic, a shoe store, and a theater that showed movies every Saturday night. In addition, in 1913, it had a large water carnival. Today it has many homes and farms, but the business district left when the Ocean Beach Highway came through in 1924.

Grays River was a busy town for longer than Deep River. It had the new highway running through it. Grays River also had two general stores, a bowling alley, a ballroom, a stage for plays, the Grange, a meat market, a garage, a restaurant, and a hotel. Today, as with Deep River, the businesses are gone.

The cannery towns along the Columbia—Altoona, Pillar Rock, and Dahlia—are all gone. The only cannery building still standing, though not used, is the Pillar Rock Cannery, now owned by Leon and Linda Gollersrud.

Knappton, also on the Columbia, was at one time one of the largest towns in Pacific County. With a population of over 300 people, it had the big mill, as well as large sailing ships and freight ships coming in to load lumber to take around the world. The mill burned in 1941. The town evacuated, leaving all the beautiful homes to fall into ruin. Today it has a beautiful scenic highway running through the town site and the old pilings still in the river. Knappton Cove still has many of the old buildings that were part of the Quarantine Station, including the hospital building, owned by Nancy Bell Anderson. Anderson has made it into an interpretive center, and it is open to the public on Saturday afternoons.

Logging has always been one of the main industries in this area, and the trees harvested in the early years were some of the largest in the world. There is still some of the old-growth forest standing. On Long Island, an island located in the Willapa Bay in Pacific County, there is a patch of old-growth cedar that wasn't burned in the fires that went through here over 500 years ago. You can only get to it by boat, with a walk of over a mile after that. The logging camps had their own cooks, mess hall, and bunk housing for the single loggers to live in. The last one to go out was the Deep River Logging Company with its train and logging camp in 1955. All the old logging camps in Grays River, Knappton, and Frankfort had their own train system to haul the logs from the woods. Some of the rivers had splash dams built in the river. They had a special way of blocking the rivers to make this kind of dam. When they released the dam, the water and the logs would wipe out everything in its path. The logs would be stopped at tidewater, rafted, and towed to a nearby mill.

In the early days, farming was a large industry. Most of the area residents lived on small and large farms, and today many of the farms have been divided into building sites for new homes.

From 1951 to 1966, Naselle had the 759th Aircraft Control and Warning Squadron/Radar Station SAGE at the Naselle Air Force Base. The Naselle Youth Camp is now located at the old base. It came in shortly after the air force base closed. The camp has been in operation for over 40 years, and it employs many people.

The schools in the area have always been very important to the people, and they still are. The school is small, but there are excellent teachers, and a large percent of area students go on to college.

Sports, especially basketball, have always been a big part of the entertainment in our community. The boys' basketball team has made more appearances at the State B Basketball Tournament in Spokane than any other school in the state of Washington. Unfortunately, they have never won the state championship, but they have won second about 10 times. Naselle-Grays River Valley School has also had good football, baseball, and track teams. The track team placed first in the state once.

Naselle hosts a Finnish-American Folk Festival every other year. This event, started in 1982, takes place the last weekend in July on even years. In 2006, Naselle was host to the International Finnish-American Festival. Many wonderful comments came from the people who attended about how much they enjoyed the small-town atmosphere.

Grays River hosts the Covered Bridge Festival every year. It takes place on the first Saturday in August. In 2007, a new park was dedicated at the site called Ahlberg Park. This park was named for the first family that owned the property. The Covered Bridge Festival is like the old-time events the area used to have many years ago.

Churches were and still are an important part of our community. They were some of the first organizations formed, many of them started with people having worship services in their homes. People of different beliefs worshipped together when the population was small. When they got larger, they would build their own denominational church.

Many fascinating people, real characters, the musically talented, artists, famous people including Ulysses S. Grant, and hardworking and just plain down-to-earth nice people have lived or visited our area over the last 150 years. I feel it a great pleasure to have lived and gone to school in this area.

One

SCHOOLS

Education was always an important part of the valley's different communities. The pioneers would start a school as soon as they were settled, usually beginning with meeting in homes. In this photograph are the Upper Grays River School children in 1899. From left to right are (first row) Benjamin Peterson, Leo Peterson, unidentified, and William Klint; (second row) Albert Swanson, Clara Johanson, Ida Swanson, teacher ? Baker, Ellen Swanson, Eleanor Klint, and Maybell Klint; (third row) Theodore Peterson, Arthur Johanson, Vesta Klint, Walter Klint, Harold Johanson, William Anderson, and Alfred Peterson.

The logging camps had their own schools in the early years. At left are students at the Olson Logging Camp on the upper Naselle River. Below is the teacher's cottage in the camp in 1919. All the houses and the school building would sit along the railroad track. When the loggers moved to a new location, the houses and the school would be loaded onto the railroad car and moved with the rest of the camp.

Riverside School was between Rosburg and Grays River on what is now the Hank and Linda Nelson farm. This picture was taken when the school was newly built in 1893. Riverside was in operation until all of Western Wahkiakum Schools consolidated into the new Rosburg School in 1938.

The Oneida School, in the 1880s, was a small building with a porch and an outhouse in the back. There were not many children who went to this school; Oneida was in a remote place along Deep River. School was held in Oneida until 1914, when all the Deep River area schools consolidated into the new Deep River School, which was located up on the hill above town.

A larger school was built in Oneida in 1893. From left to right are Emma Olson (Cornu), William Upton, Sven Svenson, Andrew Smalley, Benjamin Upton, Anita Thompson, Hilma Olson (Cornu), Elmer Upton, ? Shaw (teacher), Myrtle Smalley (Flink), Grace Upton (Bond), and Chris Bahnke.

Pictured here is the Badger School in Grays River in 1896. The children are, from left to right, (first row) Wilbur Emerson, Inez Macintosh, Adelaide Whitmore, William Baker, Lester Emerson, and Julia Lawrence; (second row) Theodore Sorenson, Frank Sorenson, Karl Lawrence, Emma Baker, Freda Anderson, Ebba Sorenson, Janet Blair, Ethel Macintosh, and Linda Ahlberg; (third row) Thomas Foss, Roy Blair, Sadie Myers, Annie Rice, Edward Rice, Edna Lawrence, Alfred Holden, Lena Whitmore, and Ida Sorenson.

This is a look into the old classrooms of the Badger School in 1899. The American flag with 46 stars hangs in front of the classroom. It appears that it may have been February because it looks as if they are studying Presidents Washington and Lincoln.

These Deep River children are on their way to school in the early 1900s. The skipper of the boat, Albin Sundberg, lived at the mouth of Deep River and picked the children up each day and brought them to school.

Twenty-one students stand with their teacher in front on the Wilme School in lower Deep River in 1901. From left to right are (first row) Eino Rangila, two unidentified girls, Eli Lassila, George Rangila, Charles Rangila, Willie Hakala, and Albert Hakala; (second row) Millie Long, Henry Wilme, Willie Long, Lena Wilme, unidentified, teacher ? Kallinen-Anderson, Elina Wirkkala, Otto Lassila, Alexander Wirkkala, Tillie Hakala, Millie Wilme, Casper Korpela, Hilia Lassila, and Anna Anderson.

The Crossroad School, in 1905, had between 20 and 30 students each year. It was located in the middle of Deep River Valley. This was the second school building in the valley. It had two teachers, one for the lower grades and one for the upper grades.

There were many schools in the area; the pioneer families felt it important to educate their children, and they would start schools in their homes almost immediately after settling. When possible, they would build a one-room schoolhouse. The children at times would have to row across a river to get to their school. Even today, education is important to the families here. The dropout rate in the Naselle-Grays River Valley School is very low, and about two-thirds of the students go onto college. The Holm School, pictured here in 1901, was one of the first schools in Naselle. From left to right are (first row) Rene Smith, Otto Parpala, Lila Smith, and Alice Holm; (second row) Tynie Parpala, Emil Erickson, Wendell Holm, Taimi Parpala, and Janfred Parpala; (third row) Florence Smith, Maud Smith, Albert Erickson, Merle Holm, and Jenny Smith.

Salmon Creek had two schools: the Upper Salmon Creek School and the Lower Salmon Creek School. This picture is of the Lower School around 1904. This school was built in the 1890s. Fifteen to 20 students attended school here most years.

This is the Maple Grove School in 1902, also known as the Upper Salmon Creek School. It looks as though there were many different ages of children. Names were not available.

This is the original Naselle Grade and High School in 1908. With the growing number of immigrants coming into the area, some with large families, the school became inadequate. By 1914, the town had added onto the school to accommodate the increasing population.

In this photograph, taken in 1914, the newly remodeled Naselle Grade and High School is featured. To the dismay of many, the old school closed in 1952. The high school was in this building until 1924, when a new high school was built.

This is the Deep River School, built in 1911. This school consolidated the Wilme School, the Oneida School, and the Crossroad School. The new school had about 50 students. It was in operation until 1938, when the new Grays River Grade School consolidated all of western Wahkiakum County into one school.

Older students are pictured at the Dahlia School in about 1934. From left to right are James Goodell, Stella Jones, Robert Jones, and Fannie Ero.

Andrew Wirkkala and his team of horses served as Naselle's first school bus. This photograph was taken in 1911. Wirkkala would pick up the children in the morning and deliver them back home in the afternoon. From the way they are dressed, it looks as if it was cold and wet out.

In the Altoona schoolyard, these girls have their picture taken with their teacher, Virginia Hansen, in about 1924. From left to right are (first row) Agnes Hendrickson, Carolyn Heiner, and Ruth Hendrickson; (second row) Elsie Heiner, Annabel Madden, Doris Bailey, teacher Virginia Hansen, and Helen Olsen.

This photograph shows the Grays River Grade School's sixth- and seventh-grade classes in 1951. From left to right are (first row) Gilbert Haataia, Wally Smalley, Duane Callos, and Ruben Koski; (second row) Phyllis Raistakka (Walker), Vivian Reed (Busse), Sally Kelly (Person), Marlene Magnuson (Montgomery), Anita Marincovich, Shirley Jackson (Magnuson), Kathleen Klint (Van Buskirk), and Mary Linn Schmand; (third row) Rodney Anderson, Donald Jones, Delores Magnuson (Smith), Diana Gollersrud (Lindstrom), Rochelle Gifford (Bonney), Edward Sotka, Wesley Raistakka, and Ronnie Jones; (fourth row) Tom Patterson, Lonnie (Stubby) Magnuson, Dean Badger, Dennis Larson, Kenny Setala, John Koski, George Haataia, Keith Olson, and teacher ? Stiener.

This is the Naselle Grade School in 1910. From left to right are (first row) Charles Moffitt; (second row) Ester Silvola (Bradburn), Arthur Niemi, Hazel Stamp, Waldemar Carlson, Ernest Koskela, Frank Oman, Esther Niemi (Gustafson), John Pernu, and Ida Oman; (third row) Bill Mickelson, Ray Hill, Saima Kolback (East), Art Heikkila, Waino Pernu, Harry Wilson, Alfred Whealdon, Ben Talus, and Adelaide McClellan; (fourth row) Heini Oman, Max Wilson, Urho Pernu, Signe Hill (Barnett), Walter Hill, and Bessie Oman (Anderson); (fifth row) teacher Pauline Poulson, Alma Niemi (Ring), Urho Wiitala, Bill Niemi, Taimi Parpala, Rowland Whealdon, and teacher Clyde Tisdale; (sixth row) Wendell Holm, Clyde Ross, Jean Davis, and Janfred Parpala.

The Naselle Grade School sixth-grade class of 1917 included, from left to right, (first row) Margaret Raemhild (Busse), Martha Hunters (Keiski), unidentified, Ester Paavola (Johnson), and unidentified; (second row) Myrtle Raemhild (Kangas), Eino Hundis, Hilja Hunters (Ruokangas), Lulu Koskela (Paavola), Hulda Penttila Bighill, Theodore Ullakko, and Aili Torppa (Niemi).

The first- and second-grade classes had their picture taken at Naselle Grade School in 1933. From left to right are (first row) Albert Raff, Reino Davis, Arvid Simukka, Warren Holm, Lawrence Ring, Albert Wirkkala, Reino Johnson, William Ehrlund, and Arvo Pollari; (second row) teacher ? Bradford, Ensie Kaimber, Mildred Wirkkala Pakenen, Nellie Penttila Kilponen, Jeanette Anderson, Elizabeth Wirkkala Lindholm, Eleanor Johnson O'Connor, Mildred Ring, and Bernice Nyberg Harkness; (third row) Annie Lindstrom Figgins, Edwin Simukka, and Lenore Nasi Larson.

The Frankfort one-room schoolhouse with an outhouse in the back is pictured here with teacher Sara Frederickson, J. B. Brandt, Nancy Brandt, Aimee Brandt, Gladys Ulfers, Lee Nelson, Virginia Hanson, Carl Hanson, and Hulda Hanson. The 1905 school year was held here from October 23, 1905, through March 16, 1906.

This picture shows a Deep River School trip at the Astor Column in 1931. Shown from left to right are (first row) Harold Haataja, Harold Manson, Carlton Appelo, Lillian Wirkkala (Zellar), Miriam Johnson (Haataia), Inez Salme (DeSemple), Emily Salme (Lunke), Elna Wirkkala (Browning), Verna Loukkola (Lechner), Signe Hanninen (Kilponen), and Venla Nikkala (Bellefeiulle); (second row) Thelma Kemppi (Strange), Dorothy Cain, Glenrose Lindgren (Hedlund), Hilda Hill (Johnson), Viola Koski (Wirkkala), and Mildred Lindgren (Jones); (third row) Edries Davis (teacher), Bob Lindgren, Harry Salme, Art Haataja (host from Astoria), Signe Wirkkala (Ellsworth), Ruth Hall (principal), unidentified host from Astoria, Cullen Baker (teacher), and unidentified host from Astoria.

Angus Bowmer taught at the Seal River School in 1927–1928. People know him across the country as the person who started the Oregon Shakespeare Festival in Ashland, Oregon. Bowmer was born in Bellingham, Washington, in 1904 and passed away in 1979. His wife, Gertrude Butler Bowman, also taught school in Seal River. She was born in 1903 and passed away in 2006.

Pictured at the Eden Valley School in 1931 are, from left to right, (first row) Robert Olson, Alma Metsala, Evelyn Sotka (Schoonover), and Alice Baxter (Wirkkala); (second row) Emily Olmstead, Alma Buskala (Simonson), Aura Metsala (Haglund), Edward Olson, Annie Olmstead, and teacher Frieda Blandon; (third row) George Durrah, Milga Sifferson (Kruse), Helen Durrah, and Aune Metsala (Tienhaara).

The New Grays River Grade School in 1938 is pictured here. Above is the interior of the new school. The photograph below was the new school, which consolidated Deep River, Altoona, Dahlia, Eden Valley, Grays River, Rosburg, and Seal River Schools. In the early 1990s, the enrollment was declining in the Naselle and Grays River Valley School District, and the school closed in 1992. All of the students now go to Naselle-Grays River Valley School in Naselle. The former school is now used for a community center.

The Fairview School in Grays River was located on Fairview Road in 1931. From left to right are (first row) Johnny Kapron, Raymond Lawrence, Virginia King (Wendelin), Maureen Meserve (Grant), Sidney Pemberton, Harry Kapron, and Edith Markland (Taft); (second row) Rose Marie Larson (Neely), Sophia Kapron (Sundahl), and Ruby Forsburg (Satterlund); (third row) Glen Markland, Agnes Agnisza Cook (Simpson), unidentified, Helen Kapron (Walker), Jacqueline "Jackie" Lawrence (Emery), Betty Heller, and Audrey Olson; (fourth row) Norman Larson, principal K. W. "Bill" Elder, teacher Belle Meade, Burtell Satterlund, Billy Klint, Evert Sorenson, Walter Kimbel, and Eugene Sorenson.

Two

FARMING THE
OLD-FASHIONED WAY

Workers at the Sam Walker farm in Grays River make hay in about 1910. The team of horses is driven by Walker from on top of the wagonload of hay. The Walkers were the first family to move into Grays River in 1866. Sam homesteaded the farm that William Meserve later owned, now owned by the Schmands.

Here Peter Dosland rides his horse on his ranch in Grays River about 1910. This picture was taken before Highway 4 (Ocean Beach Highway) went through his property. Peter was born in Norway in 1866; his wife, Mabel Olson Dosland, was born in Sweden in 1872; and they had two daughters, Pearl and Myrtle. Myrtle married George York in 1927, and they had one daughter, Corrine. Myrtle and George took over the family ranch when Myrtle's parents retired. Jon and Stephanie Gudmundsen now own it.

There were many large dairy farms in Grays River before the 1980s. This was the Meserve Farm in 1924, later owned by the Schmands. When the Meserves had the farm, most of their cows were Guernsey. The Guernsey cows are good producers of cream to make butter with; later most of the farmers went to Holstein cows, which were better suited to milk production.

This is an image of early haymaking with a gas-powered tractor. Matti Hundis rides and operates the hay rake, while his son Curly is driving the old tractor. It looks as if most of the field is nearly raked. They will use pitchforks and put the hay in shocks for easy loading on a hay wagon.

Two large work horses pull a mowing machine driven by Ole Dolson of Grays River in about 1909. The other two farmers standing by are unidentified but are more than likely farmhands of Dosland's.

Women helped their husbands with the farm work in the early years. This is Ebba Ahlberg Sorenson mowing with a team of horses in Grays River in 1912. The mowers were called a horse mower; they had about a 4-foot sickle bar and would be plugged up often from molehills and other obstacles.

A team of four work horses are pulling the plow to dig potatoes on the upper Grays River in 1915. On the other side of the horses are the many sacks of potatoes, with a crew of two men sacking them up.

This was the Christian Sorenson farm in Grays River. There was a pond on the property that had water lilies, so the farm was known as the Pond Lily Dairy. This big barn was built in 1907; Frank and Ida Sorenson Badger owned the farm after Christian, Ida's father, retired. Then it was owned by Ida's nephew and his wife, Ed and Lenore Sorenson.

Chris Sorenson built the big red barn at Pond Lily Dairy in 1907. After the hay was loaded onto the wagon and taken to the barn, workers used a pulley to put the hay on the upper level of the barn. After it was in the barn, someone would walk on the hay to pack it down so more could fit inside.

This is haymaking in Grays River Valley in 1909 on the Christian Sorenson ranch. Haying time was a busy season for the farmers; as can be seen here, all the work was done by hand. The shocks (small piles) were made over the entire field and then loaded on the wagon with just the help of a pitchfork.

Chester Laughlin plows his fields on his Grays River farm about 1910. The plow is a three-bottom plow, and it takes three workhorses to pull it. The Laughlin place later became Gus Kandoll's farm. Laughlin came to Grays River shortly after his marriage in 1904. He built and started the Dairigold Creamery in 1928.

Pictured here is old-time haymaking on the Frank Badger farm in Grays River about 1913. The hay was stacked in small piles called shocks; the crew would pick them up with pitchforks and put the shocks on the hay wagon.

Three

WHEN LOGGING WAS LOGGING

This tree, about 12 feet across, has two men lying in the cut at Deep River Timber Company in the late 1800s. The tree looks like a cedar tree, and some of the old-growth cedar trees grew very large. Cedar does not rot as some of the conifers do.

Here men log with oxen in the Sisson Creek area. Most likely it is the Brix Logging Company, as the Brix family gave this picture to the archives center. Oxen were used often in early logging; a team of oxen could pull a large log from the woods.

These are the Brix men, who had a great impact on the early days of logging in this area. They came from Germany in 1881. From left to right are (seated) the father, Peter Fredrich Brix, born in 1835; and Amus Brix, born in 1864; (standing) Albert Brix, born in 1866, who came to Grays River two years before the rest of the family; Antone Brix, born in 1877; and Peter John Brix, born in 1870.

This is the Deep River Logging Camp train moving to a new location. When the camp moved to a new location, they brought with them the housing the families lived in. They would put the houses on the train and move them from place to place. The houses would sit right next to the railroad tracks while the loggers worked a particular area.

The Olson Brothers Logging Camp mess hall shows just how many men it took to run a logging camp. There were cooks hired and women ("flunkies") to serve the meals. The dinnerware was heavy white porcelain. All of the logging companies had mess halls.

Edward Parker was a high climber, here shown up a spar tree at Deep River Logging Company. The climber would go up the tree, cutting all the limbs on the way up. He would then cut the top off the tree so the loggers could hang guy lines that would go nearly 1,000 feet or so out. The lines would be secured around stumps so the yarder could pull the logs out of the woods. The high climber was the highest paid and the most dangerous job in the woods.

The early loggers had old-growth fir timber to log, as seen by this load of logs being dumped into Grays River in 1911. The train had three logs to the load. The trees were falled (or felled) and bucked into sawmill size by a crosscut saw, which took two men to operate.

Pat Malone and Ernest Strom are falling (or felling) a large fir tree at Knappton Draw, North Shore, for the Andrew Wilson Logging Company. The crosscut saw they are using looks to be about 12 feet long.

Before the power saw came in, men used to fall (or fell) the timber with a crosscut saw, seen here at the saw shed at Saldren Logging Company in Grays River. The men who were hired to keep the saws sharpened had to be skilled in addition to well trained.

Portland Lumber Company and railroad, at the dawn of the 20th century, shows how the logging camps were laid out. The long building at the right of the picture was the mess hall; all the small buildings along the track were family housing. When it came time for the logging camp to move to a new location, they loaded the family housing on the railroad car. When a photographer came around to take pictures, the women and children all came out to be photographed as well.

The train tracks ran on the unloading dock next to the river. Here Locomotive No. 9 is coming in on a barge for Portland Lumber Company in about 1897. The unloader was used to pick up the locomotive and set it on the tracks.

Deep River Logging Train No. 7, here on its side, had just crossed over a small bridge when the train started to tip. It tipped so slowly that everyone on the train was able to get off safely. Deep River Logging Company shut down shortly after this incident in 1955. The train is now on display in Seattle.

Deep River Logging Company loggers load a log onto a locomotive by using jacks. Gus Magnuson is pictured second from the left. In front of the log is a man standing with his arm raised above him to illustrate the breadth of the log, possibly 8 or 9 feet through.

John Brix (far right) is here with his sons Herbert (standing) and John Asmus (seated on the speeder). The speeders were used on the railroad tracks for transportation. At the Deep River Logging Company, they also were used to go from family housing back in the hills into town.

This four-log load of old-growth fir logs on the Brix Brothers Logging Train in Knappton, Washington, scaled 33,756 board feet. This would build several homes. It was cut into lumber at the Knappton Mill and shipped around the world.

Mabyn Klint's house was part of a camp. Pictured here are 21 men at the Saldern Logging Camp at the bottom of KM Mountain in Grays River, Washington. Included here are Henry Holden, Ed Malone, Ben Peterson, Hjalmer Klint, Tony Anderson, Andrew Anderson, Carl Erickson, Pat Malone, Victor Anderson, Walter Anderson, Martin Olson, Willie Hakala, John Nelson, Kaarlo Mikkola, Jack Schwendin, Ludwig Satterlund, and Pete Larson.

Fred Stackpole was the engineer of the Saldren Logging Company's Locomotive No. 2 from Grays River. Three days after this picture was taken in 1899, Stackpole was killed while on a runaway train.

Engine No. 9 brought in a load of logs to be dumped in Grays River. Men were riding on the top of the load as it came in. Note the length of the train.

A Deep River Logging Company train crosses over a deep ravine on a trestle made from logs that were 75–100 feet long. It is amazing the loggers were able to construct such a difficult feat. This type of construction was called "single pole" trestle. It looks as though the trees have had the bark removed to help keep the rot out. This type of railroad building is now likely a lost art.

A Deep River Logging Company train dumps its load of logs in 1912. As the picture shows, the logs were huge and mostly in three-log loads. The camp operated at Deep River from before 1900 to 1955, when Deep River Logging shut down. The metal tracks went to India for termite-proof telephone poles, and the bell is on display at Disneyland.

The Grays River Shake Mill was located on the Grays River in Rosburg, Washington. Theodore Swanson Sr. originally built the mill in 1911. It burned down in 1920. After it burned, Johnny Johnson came on as a partner to Swanson. There were several different kinds of shakes produced at the mill, first the Gloria Brand, then the Florence Brand, and later the Ted's Brand. These brands were all named for Swanson's children. The mill closed in 1939. Swanson then started Grays River Logging Company.

The No. 4 train from Grays River is loaded with old-growth fir. Most of the logs are 5 to 6 feet through. Trains were used in most of the logging areas in the early days. This picture was taken sometime around the dawn of the 20th century.

In 1910, the Deep River Logging Company constructed a 650-foot tunnel at a cost of $54,000. Twelve million board feet of timber was used to shore up the tunnel. The timbers were cut at the new sawmill, located in the town of Deep River. The elimination of the adverse grade made it possible to expand Deep River Logging Company into the Salmon Creek Valley.

This is a camp on the lower Naselle River of the Spruce Division, used in World War I. The government recruited loggers to get out spruce timber for the manufacture of airplanes. Later on, soldiers were employed; they stayed in their own camps, took extra training, and worked with the loggers. Thirty-thousand soldiers served in the Spruce Division. By the time the war ended, the spruce lumber production was averaging 12 million board feet a month.

Fall Creek Dam #98

Splash dams were used on the Naselle River in the late 1800s and early 1900s to move the logs down the river. A large dam was built in the river to form a lake of about three acres. It took about three weeks for the lake to fill up. Before the loggers would let the dam go, they would go down the river and warn all the families that they were going to let the logs come down the river. The logs came down with a great force and pretty much destroyed everything in their path. Once down to the tidewater, loggers would raft the logs, and the tugboat would pull the rafts to the mill.

Sunshine, Washington 1887–1897.
on Shoal Water Bay (Willapa Bay)

Sunshine, Washington, was destined to be a large town; it was located near the mouth of the Naselle River, where the river flowed into Willapa Bay. It had deep water so the ships could get in and out easily. A sailing ship was in at the mill when this picture was taken. The town was vacated before the start of the 20th century. There was a large hotel and saloon built in the town and never used. The Pioneer Lutheran Church of Deep River bought the building in 1897 for $2.50, tore it down, and built the church. They sold the leftover lumber for $50.

An unusual picture shows a group of young women sitting in the cut of a tree at the Pete Morrell Logging Company. The timber fallers at the base of the tree are Ash Feazle (left) and Samuel Feazle. From left to right are (at the base of the tree) Maggie Ahlberg; (on the first springboard) Ellen Swanson (Larson); (on the next springboard) Alma Swanson (Etters); (seated in the undercut) Linda Ahlberg (Feazle), Julia Lawrence (Durrah), Ebba Ahlberg (Sorenson), and Annie Rice.

James Houston Vaughn, born in 1836, built the Knappton Mill on the Columbia River in 1869 for J. B. Knapp and S. E. Barr. Later Asa M. Simpson owned and operated the mill. The Peter F. Brix family bought the mill in 1909. The Deep River Logging Company was the last to own the mill before it burned on July 12, 1941. Knappton had grown to be one of the largest towns in Pacific County with over 300 residents. All that remains today is the piling in the river where the mill once stood and a scenic highway, built in 1960, running through the area.

August Heldt, the operator of this steam donkey for North Shore Logging Company, is pictured here in about 1914.

Eastern and Western Logging Company Engine No. 6 hauls logs through a beautiful stand of timber along the Columbia River around 1900. Two men stand near the tracks, and two are on top of the load of logs. Eastern and Western logged in the Grays River area for many years.

Victor and Edward Habakangas are pictured at the Olson Brother Logging Camp blacksmith shop in Salmon Creek. All the logging camps had their own blacksmith shops in the early days. It was a vital part of operations, and these men were trained to make any part that would break.

Ralph Olmstead, driving a Spargo truck, hauls for Barr and Lindros Logging Company in 1955. Logs as big as these came through Grays River for many years.

This is the crew at the Knappton Mill in 1880. There was a large crew, and many of the men and families spoke different languages, such as Finnish, Swedish, Polish, and German. These men and their families had to overcome many obstacles to converse with one another.

A broad view of Knappton town and the mill in 1913 is pictured here. The mill is in the distance with two large ships in to load up with lumber. The buildings in the middle of the picture against the hill are the store and the community hall. A boardwalk went between all the businesses and homes.

Weyerhaeuser started logging in the Grays River area about 1955. They hauled into the Deep River sorting yard, where the logs were sorted then rafted in the river, and the tugboats hauled them to the mills. Weyerhaeuser closed their operations in the area in August 1983 and sold the yard. It is now being used to chip small logs that come into the yard.

John Haglund and Walt Paavola are sitting on top of this cut log of old-growth fir with a Weyerhaeuser logging crew in Grays River, Washington, in 1957. Also shown are, from left to right, (first row) Jules Conrad, George Fauver, and Charlie Keiski; (second row) Slim Blankenship, Brian Salme, Ray Ervest, John Bighill, and Otto Keiski.

Four

EARLY TRANSPORTATION, FISHING, AND BOATS

The original name for Naselle was Nasel, a Native American name. This is the landing on the Nasel River around 1910. The ferry was the *Greyhound*, and the landing was a link to the outside world in the early years. All the mail came from Nachotta, and most of the supplies came through South Bend, the county seat of Pacific County. It was a two-day trip to South Bend by boat. Today it takes about half an hour by car.

William Hume, with his brothers George, Joseph, and Robert, established the first salmon cannery on the Columbia River in 1866 at Eagle Cliff, Washington. They went on to own half of the 35 canneries on the lower Columbia River. In 1881, they submitted Eagle Cliff brand canned salmon for judging in competition in England. The quality was so good that they won a gold medal for excellence from Queen Victoria. This cannery packed 4,000 cases during its first year of operation. In 1867, some 18,000 cases were packed. William Hume was also an avid sportsman; he loved to hunt and fish around Eagle Point and Hume Station (later called Altoona). Hume also built the first salmon cannery on the Sacramento River in 1864.

The Altoona Packing Company was located on the Columbia River and was only accessible by boat. The cannery was built in 1903 and operated until 1947; it employed many people throughout those years. In 1998, a strong windstorm hit the Washington coast; the remnants of the cannery fell into the Columbia River as a result.

Fishermen used these net racks at the Pillar Rock Cannery, on the Columbia River, around the beginning of the 20th century. The fishermen continue today, racking their nets the same as in the olden days; they carefully go through each net, inspecting it for torn spots. Any torn spots are mended by hand.

The Pillar Rock Cannery in Pillar Rock, Washington, began operations in 1879 by Richard Everding and Sylvester Farrell, canning 300 cases of salmon the first year and increasing production every year. The first people to work at the cannery were Chinese; in later years, they hired women. There were not any roads into Pillar Rock. The only way to get to the cannery was by boat. The building is now owned by Linda and Leon Gollersrud.

The Pillar Rock Cannery was known to have several feet of salmon on the floor. In the early days, this was a common sight at the canneries as salmon was very plentiful. The man looking on from the right side is Bud Harrington, manager of the cannery.

In the 1800s, the Finns and Swedes brought the fish trap idea to the Columbia River. Piling was put in a circle, and nets were put around the piling to make fish traps. There were around 400 of these fish traps on the Columbia River. The people who fished this way were very successful, although the method was unpopular with the gillnet fishermen. Eventually the practice was outlawed.

A Mr. Parnell (left), the bookkeeper at the Klevenhusen cold storage plant in Altoona, and Otto Larson pose on the dock of the Altoona Packing Company with a 73-pound chinook salmon. The largest salmon ever caught was 95 pounds, captured by one of the area's Native Americans.

The *Martha*, owned by the Klevenhusen Packing Company, is held fast by the ice during a record-breaking cold weather in January 1930, when the Columbia River froze over. This picture was taken from the docks in Altoona, Washington.

This upriver view of Cottardi Station and net racks reveals the Altoona Packing Company in the distance. Life on the river was never lonely and always busy, even though boat transportation was the only way to get there.

The *Julia B.* was a passenger boat that took passengers from Grays River, Deep River, Cathlamet, Skamokawa, and Knappton to Astoria. It usually made the trip each day.

The Astoria–Knappton–Deep River ferry, *The Pioneer,* is pictured in the early 1900s. This ferry was the first to haul passengers and cars across the Columbia River.

The W. N. Meserve store in Grays River welcomed *The Butte* and its passengers in 1913. The store continued to operate until Highway 4 was opened.

Here are two of the large ferries that came into local rivers at the dawn of the last century. These two boats are the *Wenona* and the *Ottowa*; both made regular runs to Grays River, Rosburg, Deep River, Knappton, and Astoria.

The *General Washington* leaves the dock in Deep River about 1910. It has passed the Shamrock Hotel with its many passengers on board; it would make stops at Frankfort and Knappton, ending its voyage in Astoria.

A small mail boat and passenger boat, the *Nachotta*, goes under the steel bridge in Naselle built in 1907. One can see many passengers on the boat, the women dressed in long skirts and some of the men in suits.

Wind-powered sail fishing boats (the Butterfly Fleet) sailed on the Columbia River. Pictured here in 1902 is a boat belonging to the Cottardi fishing village in Cottardi, Washington. The boat was the *May*.

The passenger boat the *Mayflower* sails here on the Columbia River with a wind-powered fishing boat of the Butterfly Fleet behind it. It is easy to see by the size of the larger boat how small the boats of the Butterfly Fleet were.

This is the *Queen* leaving Rosburg on October 5, 1911, to take Emil and Johanna Amundsen Kandoll on their wedding trip to get married in Cathlamet, Washington. Many people were on the boat making this trip. Emil and Johanna had five children born to them: the first child (1912) was stillborn, Ernest (1915), Mabel Kandoll Herold (1916), Walter (1921), and Richard (1926).

Johanna Amundsen Kandoll rows her boat on the Grays River to local doings (possibly a baby shower, wedding, or to church) in the Rosburg area. She is dressed in her finest wear for the occasion.

The *Victoria* was owned and operated by the Hoikka family of Rosburg, Washington. The *Victoria* made daily trips between Grays River and Astoria. One of the captains on the *Victoria* was Jennie Hoikka Pearson, now 94 years young and with many wonderful stories to tell.

Jennie Kristina Hoikka was born February 25, 1914, in Centerville, Washington. She was the seventh of 14 children born to Charles and Anna Lehto Hoikka, immigrants from Finland. She married Elvin Pearson, an immigrant from Sweden, in 1935. They had two children: Donald and Judy Pearson Jones.

Five

OUR PEOPLE

The William Nelson Meserve family, shown in 1910, included, from left to right, Solomon (born 1906), Imogene (born 1901), W. N. (born 1867), and Alta Harriet (Smith), born 1878. Two more children were born to the Meserves after this photograph was taken. The Meserve family had much influence on the Grays River area: they owned a large store, William Nelson Meserve was a surveyor, and Alta Harriet Meserve was a schoolteacher before she married. She also owned and published the newspaper *Grays River Builder* for many years. It was the Meserves who worked to get Highway 4 from Longview to Long Beach put in.

A family gathering of the Barr and Vaughn families in Grays River takes place in 1906. From left to right are (first row) May Vaughn and Adelaide Barr; (second row) Bill Vaughn, Leonard Vaughn, Cyrus Vaughn, Thad Barr, Phoebe Barr, Louise Barr, and Ruth Barr; (third row) Edith Vaughn, Mildred Vaughn, Annie Vaughn, George Houston Vaughn, Olive Barr, Ras Barr, Margaret Barr, Jessie Barr, W. L. Barr, Willie Barr, and Dewitt Barr.

The Bighill family homestead on the upper Naselle River is seen here. From left to right are Bill, born 1885; Charles, 1887; Henry, 1889; Otto, 1890; Oscar, 1895; Albert, 1898; father Lee, born in Finland in 1859; baby Jenny, 1901; mother Fiina, born in Finland in 1864; and Olga, 1884. Three more children were born to the Bighill family: Ester, 1901; Walt, 1903; and Ellen, 1905. Many of Lee Bighill's descendants still live in the Naselle area.

John and Georgiana Grimes Beare were from Mississippi and Missouri and married in 1909; they purchased a 40-acre farm near Brookfield, Washington. They virtually shut themselves off from the outside world for the next 32 years, living off the land. They raised their own fruit, meat, and vegetables. John Beare made a few trips to the outside world, but Georgiana never left the place until 1929, when she had to travel to Cathlamet on legal business. She wore her 20-year-old wedding clothes, which made quite an impression on folks. John had a paralytic stroke and died in a local hospital in 1941. The aged widow was persuaded to leave her 11 head of cattle, her dried beans and sacks of apples stored for winter, and come out the second time in her wedding clothes; she was 80 years old. She entered the nursing home in Cathlamet and lived until she was a couple of days short of her 96th birthday.

Around the dawn of the 20th century, the Huntus brothers emigrated from Finland to Naselle. What made these four brothers stand out was the fact that they did not want anybody to get confused about who they were, so they each took a different spelling for their name. They were Matti Hundis, John Huntus, Charles Hunters, and Andrew Hundus.

Matti and Matilda Lindstrom Hundis are pictured here with their two oldest children, Rahua and Curley, and Grandma Marijana Winturr Lindstrom in 1906. The Hundis home was one of the first homes in Naselle and was built by Isaac Lane. The home is now owned by Jon and Megan Tienhaara.

The Smalley family of Rocky Point and Eden Valley had this portrait taken in the 1890s. From left to right are (seated) Megan Ann Magan Smalley, born 1835; Myrtle Smalley Flink, 1880; James Andrew Smalley, 1828; and Sarah Smalley Larson, 1874; (standing) Florence Smalley Hansen, 1869; Frank Smalley, 1867; Edna Smalley Upton, 1857; and Alice Smalley Parcher, 1865.

One of the pioneer families of Eden Valley was that of Elmer Durrah. Here from left to right are (first row) George, born 1919; Mary Jane Adams Durrah, 1859 (Elmer's mother); and Helen, 1917; (second row) Elmer, 1886; Harold, 1915; and Nellie Larson Durrah, who came from Kansas to teach school in Eden Valley. Grandmother Mary Jane Adams Durrah was related to John Adams, John Quincy Adams, and Jefferson Davis.

This is an 1899 photograph of Frank Badger and his sweetheart Ida Sorenson as he teaches her to ride a bicycle. Looking on is Ida's brother Frank Sorenson.

Frank and Ida Sorenson Badger are pictured here on their wedding day, December 25, 1902. Frank and Ida were a very popular and colorful couple in the Grays River area. They owned and operated a large farm, the Pond Lily Dairy, for many years. Frank and Ida had three children—Hazel, Art, and Harold. There are many descendants of this family still in the area.

Deep River and Naselle women are spinning, knitting, and embroidering at the home of Fiina Bjork Lindy Koski. From left to right are Laura Nasi, Sylvia Nasi, Antti Anolta, Jenny Lindy, Helmi Lindy, Helga Nasi, Hilda Lindy, Viola Koski Wirkkala, and Fiina Bjork Lindy Koski. Eight former Naselle High School students meet for a little reunion below. They are from left to right as follows: (first row) Bessie Oman Anderson, born 1896; Annie Oman Wiitala, 1892; Tekla Kolback Wirkkala, 1888; Milga Kolback Wirkkala, 1892; and Winnie Oman Hall, 1888; (second row) Saima Kolback East, 1898; Signe Hill Barnett, 1895; and Ester Silvola Bradburn, 1895.

The Emil Lindgren family of Deep River is pictured here. From left to right are (first row) Glenrose Lindgren Hedlund, Dianne Hedlund, Lillian Johnson Lindgren, and little Elaine Hedlund in front; (second row) Ivan Jones, Mildred Lindgren Jones, Emil Lindgren, and Irwin Jones.

The Wilme family posed in front of their Deep River home in 1906. Many of the homes were large like the Wilme house; the Wilmes had eight children. On their property was a school called the Wilme School. Near the house was Deep River, and the area was called Wilme's Landing. In the early days, Salmon Creek people got their supplies from the boats that came into Wilme's Landing.

John and Helen Andresen Johnson were married in 1901. This picture was taken in about 1906. Their youngest boy, Harold, was born in 1904, and Earl was born in 1902. The Johnsons homesteaded and farmed in Rosburg. Their great-grandson Earl Johnson has the place now and runs beef cattle.

These are the adult children of pioneers Frank Benjamin Hull and Sarah McCoon Hull of Grays River. They are, from left to right, (first row) Ella Hull Sorenson, 1861; Clara Hull Durrah, 1863; and Julia Hull Powell, 1872; (second row) William, born 1869; Joseph, 1875; and Charles, 1865. This photograph was taken around 1910. Many offspring of this family are still residents of Wahkiakum County.

The children of Frank Badger and Ida Sorenson Badger are on an outing to Seaside in 1920. From left to right are Harold Badger, age 9; Arthur Badger, age 13; and Hazel Badger Elder, age 16.

Here in 1928 are four generations of the Badger and Sorenson families. From left to right are (seated) George Wesley Badger holding Rodney Badger, who died at one year of age, and Ella Hull Sorenson holding Marjorie Elder Kraxberger; (standing) Frank Badger, Art Badger, Hazel Badger Elder, and Ida Sorenson Badger.

Pictured here is the 1919 funeral of Cpl. William Barr, who was wounded in France in World War I, was taken to a hospital in New York, and passed away there. Corporal Barr was born in 1893 in Grays River. The above picture shows the hearse pulled by a team of horses. Below, the army waits at the Grays River Methodist Church for the casket to come out.

Norman Schuler, from Naselle; his wife, Hilda Koskela Schuler; and their daughter Genita are pictured in the fall of 1936. Norman was one of the early causalities of World War II when the ship he was on went down in the South Pacific. Norman owned the store in Naselle that later became Appelo's. Hilda later married Urho Wirkkala.

The Paju family of Deep River is a typical Finnish immigrant family. Most of the families in the late 19th and early 20th centuries in Deep River and Naselle were hardworking Finnish people. From left to right are (first row) Pearl Paju Mattson, born 1904; Celia Paju Hill, 1909; and Edvard Paju (father), 1874; (second row) Bertha Paju Pyhtila, 1901; Emma Lauren Paju (mother), 1878; and Agnes Paju Appelo, 1899.

The Jonathan Green Elliott family, shown here in 1895, lived at Elliott's Landing on the Columbia River. Pictured from left to right are (seated) Jonathan Green Elliott, born 1832; Agnes Ducheney Elliott, 1852; and Grandma Mary Rondeau Ducheney Kelly (granddaughter of Chief Comcomly); (standing) Eliza Elliott, 1880; Charles Elliott, 1873; Harry Lavery; Grace Elliott, 1878; Grant Elliott, 1888; unidentified; Joseph Elliott, 1885; and William Elliott, 1869. Grant Elliott was named for Ulysses S. Grant.

Included in this group of children at Charles Moffitt's 12th birthday party in 1915 are, from left to right, (first row) Thomas O'Connor, Locksley Whealdon, Waldemar Carlson, Theodore Higgins, William O'Connor, Bill Higgins, Forrest Holm, and Francis O'Connor; (second row) Frank Oman, Harry Wilson, Charles Moffitt, Ralph Wilson, Alfred Whealdon, Virginia Carlson, Lucille Moffitt, and Lucille Carlson.

The John Hill family of Naselle, pictured from left to right in about 1907, are (seated) John, Otto, and Liisa (John's wife); (standing) Walter, Werner, Lempi Hill Nyman, Elizabeth "Betty" Hill Bighill, Signe Hill Barnette, and Ray.

This is a 1919 picture taken in Knappton after a McAllister/ Chadwick family trip to Long Beach digging clams. From left to right are Glenn McAllister holding daughter Marian (McAllister) Lindros, Dexter McAllister, Lorena (Erp) Chadwick, Lorena's daughter Eleanor (Chadwick) Reany, Carrie (Wells) McAlister, and Ruth (Barr) McAllister.

Otto and Milga Kolback Wirkkala are pictured on their wedding day, June 1, 1912. They made their home in Naselle and had five children. Their first child, Alice, was born and died in 1913, followed by Richard, born 1914; Mildred Wirkkala Pakanen, born 1918; Anna Wirkkala Ehrlund, born 1921; and Robert Wirkkala, born 1928. Anna still lives in Naselle; there are many descendants of this couple in the area.

On the steps of their Grays River home are John and Anna Neilson Swanson in about 1912. John was a logger and had his own logging company. Anna and John were both born in Sweden, John in 1852 and Anna in 1858; they married in 1880. There were eight children born to them: Teddy Swanson, born 1882; Rudolph Swanson, 1884; Albert Swanson, 1886; Ellen Swanson Larson, 1887; Ida Swanson Larson, 1889; Ruth Swanson Markland, 1892; Alma Swanson Etters, 1897; and Edith Swanson, 1899.

The Brix family was all born in Germany. They immigrated to the United States in 1881. This 1886 portrait of the John Peter Brix family shows, from left to right (seated) Peter John, born 1870; Maria Andreson Brix, 1840; Herman, 1878; Peter Fredrick, 1835; Amus, 1864; and Albert, 1866; (standing) Helen "Lena," 1875; Christopher, 1872; Margaret "Maggie," 1866; and Antone, 1877. The Brix family with their business abilities started out logging and then bought the Knappton Mill in 1909. They also had the Knappton Tow-boat Company, which hauled mostly rafts of logs to the mills, and some of the family is still in business today.

Some of Naselle's teenagers in about 1918 take time out to pose for a picture. They are, from left to right, (first row) Victor Ullakko, Otto Hill, and Charles Keiski, all born in 1903; (second row) Anna Anderson, Linnea Ehrlund Ullakko (born 1904), Helmie Penttila (born 1902), and Olga Silvola (born 1902).

The John and Maria Bjork Silvola family of Naselle is pictured in about 1936. John was born in 1876 and Maria was born in 1869, both in Finland. The couple married in 1894 and came to America in 1898. They were the parents of nine children.

Luke and Lottie Durrah Kimbel are seen here on their wedding day—August 8, 1908—in Grays River. The Kimbels had five children, with three of them living to be adults: Melvin Kimbel, Opal Kimbel Kraft, and Walter Kimbel.

Six

INTERESTING PLACES, HOMES, AND BUSINESSES

The first settlers to come to Naselle were Irish—the Whealdons in 1863 and the O'Connors in 1870. The first Finns to come were in 1875, followed by many Finnish families, who took out homesteads. This image is a view of Naselle in 1910 from Chapman Hill (the Paul Wirkkala farm). The home on the far left is still standing; also the home on the far right in the distance (Kandoll Farm) is still in use. The view of Naselle is very different today.

Pillar Rock sits out in the Columbia River about 1,000 feet; it stands about 25 feet above water and about 100 feet below water. A few great people have seen the rock, including Lewis and Clark on their expedition to find the Pacific Ocean. In addition, Ulysses S. Grant spends considerable time in the Pillar Rock area, as he was friends with the Jonathan Green Elliott family. In 1922, the Corps of Engineers in conjunction with the Light House Services dynamited the top off the rock to place a beacon on it.

The Grays River Covered Bridge is the last covered bridge in the state of Washington. The construction of the bridge took place in 1905, and it was covered in 1906. It is 158 feet long and 14 feet wide. At the site of the covered bridge each year on the first Saturday in August, an old-time country festival takes place. In 2007, a new park, the Ahlberg Park, was dedicated in honor of the first people to own the land.

This picture is of a landmark called the "Four Trees"; it is on the west end of Altoona and marks the site of an old Native American burial ground. It was used in the days when the Native Americans had exclusive use of the site.

The swinging bridges were the only way people had of getting across the rivers in the early days, as there were not any roads. Naselle and Grays River had several on the river. This swinging bridge was the Bighill swinging bridge across the Naselle River. There is still one swinging bridge left, the Bergquist Swinging Bridge on the upper Naselle River.

The Grays River Falls is located in the gorge on the Grays River. In 1905, W. N. Meserve was logging in the area of the falls, which were so high the fish could not get up the river to spawn. Meserve had the falls blasted. In the late 1940s, when Wirkkala brothers were logging in the area, the Department of Fisheries blasted the falls for the second time. A man was killed from the blast.

Grays River is known for its flooding. The flood in this picture was in 1909, when the town and the fields went underwater. Grays River has flooded its banks nearly every year known to modern man.

William and Harriet Meserve of Grays River had a vision. They built this bowling alley on the top floor of their new store when they remodeled in 1909. It had two lanes, and it was an exciting new addition for this remote town only accessible by boat. They also added a barbershop, a ballroom, and a large stage where the communities would put on plays. A few apartments were added to the back of the building.

The U.S. Public Health Quarantine Station at Knappton Cove on the Columbia River was constructed in 1899 and closed in 1938. Thousands of European and Asian immigrants, lured to the Pacific Northwest by the salmon and timber industries, passed through a U.S.–required health inspection at this port of entry. The effective control of communicable diseases in the lower Columbia River area is attributed to the station's work. The old hospital building is now an interpretive center, open from Memorial Day through Labor Day on Saturdays from 1:00 to 4:00 p.m.

The town of Knappton at the dawn of the 20th century was a busy town, with a sawmill and a deepwater port. The building to the center right is the hotel, and next to the hotel on the right is the general store, with a row of small houses for the workers to live in. Going up the hill is the long boardwalk that connected the houses to the lower part of the town, with many homes along the way.

"The Rukoushuone" (Naselle Prayer House) was once the Whealdon School. The structure was moved to the corner of the Hill Farm in 1908, when all the Naselle-area schools consolidated. The Rukoushuone was nondenominational and served all Naselle residents. Only Finnish was spoken in this church, as nearly all the residents of Naselle were Finnish. Services were held here until 1928, when the Congregationalists and the Lutherans built their own church.

The Finnish Lutherans of Deep River and Salmon Creek built the Deep River Pioneer Church in 1898–1899; in 2004, the outside of the church was lovingly restored. The inside is all original with a wine glass pulpit, wooden benches, and a large oil painting hanging on the front wall of the church. The same heater has heated the church for over 100 years and still heats it. Many weddings and special occasions, and occasionally a funeral, still take place at the old church. It is on the National Register of Historic Places.

A large crowd gathered for the dedication of the Congregational United Church of Christ in 1928. At first, only Finnish services were held, as most of the residents of Naselle were from Finland. The church is still going strong, with many of the original native families attending.

On January 2, 1906, the Naselle women formed the Naselle Finnish Sewing Circle. They bought a schoolhouse the district no longer needed, and they were devout toward missions and hospitals. During World War I, they supported the Red Cross with the war effort. The Sewing Circle ended in 1977. Pictured in 1906 are, from left to right, (first row) Lulu (Koskela) Paavola, Pearl Koskela, and Rauha Silvola; (second row) Aliina (Kentala) Niemi, Maija Korpela, Ida Talus, Tilda Koskela, Adeline Chapman, Sandra (Korpela) Wirkkala, Minnie (Paavola) Pakanen, baby Grace Pakanen, Hilda (Korpela) Wirkkala holding Howard Wirkkala Sr.; and Olga (Korpela) Timonen.

This is one of the fine homes built in Knappton about 1870. The family that lived in this home the longest called it Crescent Mound. There were a large number of homes in the area overlooking the Columbia River and the Knappton Mill. When the mill burned in 1941, the town of Knappton and this lovely old home were abandoned.

Thomas George Washington O'Connor built the O'Connor house in 1918. O'Connor and his wife, Clara Collins O'Connor, raised six children in this beautiful home. Many community events took place here in the early days. This picture was taken during a freshet from the old Naselle River Bridge. Walter and Ruth Maki Anderson have owned the home for many years.

The Randolph Durrah House in Grays River was a Sears home; all the supplies were purchased from Sears. Many have thought it was a Sears kit, but they did not come out until 1908, and this house was built in 1896. It sits on top of a hill overlooking the valley and the river. This lovely old home passed to Randolph Durrah's son, and the last Durrah to live in the house was his grandson. The new owners have remodeled the house and restored it as close as they could to its former glory.

The Antone Klint family stands in front of their newly remodeled home in Grays River in 1895. Pictured from left to right are Walter Klint, born 1888; Hjalmar Klint, 1873 (brother to Antone); Maybell Klint, 1886; Eleanor Klint, 1884; Antone Klint, 1848; Hannah Mansson Klint, 1852, holding Carrie Klint, 1895; Mildred Klint, 1882; William Klint, 1888; and Vesta Klint, 1890. Antone and Hannah were both born in Sweden; Antone came to the United States in 1890.

The Nasel Hotel at Nasel Landing was built in 1889. It was a popular sportsman's resort, and wild game was served at the meals. By 1918, the Thomas Carlson family owned the hotel and renamed it the Carlson Hotel. They are pictured here from left to right: Virginia Carlson, Lucille Carlson, Waldemar Carlson, Thomas and Julia Penttila Carlson, and Harvey Carlson.

Nasel Post Office is shown here in 1910. The first post office was established in 1877, discontinued in 1878, and reestablished again in 1881. In 1921, Nasel was changed to Naselle. Thomas George Washington O'Connor is out front with the team of horses; his wife, Clara, is seated on the right holding their daughter Katherine; their boys Tom, Francis, and Bill stand next to their mother.

Charles A. Niemi poses in front of his store in 1919. The store was located near Naselle Landing, at the end of the South Fork River. The bridge railing is visible on the left of the picture, and all merchandise was brought in by boat. Next to Niemi's store was the blacksmith shop owned and operated by Oscar Timonen.

Naselle's first taxi, seen in the early 1900s, was owned and driven by Andrew Wirkkala. Wirkkala married Tekla Kolback in 1909, and they had five children. Later they moved to Ilwaco and made that their permanent home.

Luke Kimbel made daily trips delivering supplies between Grays River and Deep River. One day, things did not go according to plan, and Kimbel ended up in the Deep River. This is the ferry the *General Washington* pulling Kimbel's delivery wagon out of the river.

Appelo's bought the Red and White Store in 1934. They had a full line of groceries, hardware, clothing, and boots. They carried Standard Oil products and U.S. Tires and had big signs on the outside of the store for John Deere products. The Grays River Post Office was also housed in the store. C. A. and Agnes Appelo owned stores in Deep River and Naselle as well.

Grays River in the early part of the 1900s was a good-sized town. The Peterson Hotel was a main part of the town, as there were many outside people who came in to do business, hunt, and fish. The Peterson was built before 1910.

The Shamrock Hotel in Deep River is pictured in 1927 behind, from left to right, Fred Pentti, ? Larson, and Andrew Mattson. The Finnish Steam Bath is on the right. The Shamrock's builder, Charles Swhwegler, named the hotel after a riverboat that had made daily trips between Deep River and Astoria, Oregon. Swhwegler purchased a parcel of land from the Deep River Land and Wharf Company in 1903 and erected a building used for other purposes until 1914, when Nestor and Hulda Wirkkala purchased it for a hotel. They ran it for more than 20 years, and their son and daughter-in-law Charles and Ellen Wirkkala ran it until 1956. In 1977, the building was torn down.

Pictured here is Pentti's Pool Hall in Deep River in 1929. Pentti lost an arm and a leg in a logging accident working on the train; the loggers took up a collection and bought him this pool hall, a very popular hangout in the early days. Pentti was born in Finland in 1893. He fell down a flight of stairs in his pool hall and died in 1946. With Pentti (left) are, from left to right, Burton Appelo, C. A. Appelo, and Carlton Appelo.

Helge Saari, born in Finland in 1898, was the father of Vivian Saari Smalley and Darlene Saari Haataja. Helge delivered milk to Altoona residents for many years; he delivered at low tide, as he would have to go along the beach from his farm to the town of Altoona with a small trailer pulled by his horse. Helge did this for many years.

Tom Carlson is seen driving Naselle's first freight truck in 1911. He hauled freight and passengers between Naselle and Knappton. It looks like some of the boys rode bicycles to school, as they are standing in the back of the bus with their bicycles. The students, in no particular order, are Linnea Ehrlund, Annie Bighill, Virginia Carlson, and Waldemar Carlson.

The newspaper office in Frankfort, Washington, on the Columbia River was located here in 1880. Frankfort was a busy town with fishing and logging. Residents had hoped to get the train to come into the town, but it never did, and the town slowly died out. There was never a road to Frankfort; it was only accessible by water.

Ole Dosland, a farmer from Grays River, had the contract to build Ocean Beach Highway in 1922. This picture shows the farmers hard at work on the road just west of the town of Grays River.

Seven

SPORTS, FESTIVALS, AND FUN

The Wahkiakum County Fair celebrates 100 years in 2008. Grays River Grange started the Wahkiakum County Fair in 1908, when it was held in Grays River. In 1912, it moved to Skamokawa so it would be more centrally located in the county. This beautiful display was at the Grays River fair in 1910.

Men, women, and children line the bridge and the boat for the Deep River Water Carnival in 1913. The water carnival was held for several years in the early part of the century. Many different events took place, like foot racing on the boardwalk.

Deep River is a swampy marsh area, and when the tide came in, the town was under water. Boardwalks were built to enable people to move around freely. Charles Rangila started building dikes in 1911 to keep the high tides off his farmland. In the early days, Deep River was a very busy town, with the railroad bringing logs in to be rafted and shipped to the mills in Astoria, Oregon, or in Knappton. Passenger boats came in every day to deliver mail, supplies, and passengers. At right, on the hill, was the theater that showed movies on Saturday evenings. People would bring their lanterns and come from miles around. This picture was taken at the 1913 Water Festival in Deep Water.

In the summer months, dances were held on the Ullakko Bridge with the music of an accordion player. People came from Knappton and Naselle to attend these dances. This particular dance was in 1911 for the Brix Logging Camp picnic.

From left to right, Wendell Holm and Janfred Parpala ride bicycles around Naselle in 1913, the year they were part of the first graduating class from Naselle High School. Parpala went on to become a doctor, and Holm was in the oyster business and had a large dairy farm in Naselle.

A celebration of the opening of the highway from Kelso to Ocean Beach took place in 1924 on the Thomas O'Connor farm in Naselle. One of the events of the day was judging cattle, as shown in this photograph.

The folks in Deep River and Naselle would all get together in a centrally located place and celebrate special occasions. Here they are celebrating the Fourth of July in 1910 at the Wilme place in Deep River.

The children of Knappton mark the Fourth of July 1919 celebration with a parade of their wagons and tricycles all decorated with flowers and greenery. They marched all the way down the long boardwalk and posed for a picture.

The Grays River Covered Bridge Festival in 1995 shows how loggers went up a tree to fall (or fell) it using springboards and an axe. The festival takes place each year on the first Saturday of August. It includes many logging demonstrations, a petting zoo, and a good time with lots of good things to eat.

Naselle Kentala Players play for the Finnish-American Folk Festival. This festival is the last Saturday of July in even years at the Naselle School. The Kentala is a popular instrument in Finnish culture. The music is soothing and mellow. The musicians are, from left to right, Wiljo Saari, May Saari Adair, and Laurie Wirkkala. In 2006, Wiljo Saari was awarded the National Heritage Fellowship for the Folk and Traditional Arts Program of the National Endowment for the Arts.

The loggers' picnic is held each July in Deep River. This picture was taken about 1970; Theodore Swanson Sr. is playing the violin.

Fishing has always been a favorite pastime for people in the Naselle-Grays River Valley, since both the Naselle River and the Grays River are excellent fishing rivers. This picture shows young men fishing on the upper Naselle River rapids in 1908; they are, from left to right, Oscar Nyberg, Albert Penttila, Otto Wirkkala, and Otto Bighill.

In the early years, the Grays River Grange would put plays on for everyone to come and enjoy. This particular play, *The New Minister*, was performed by members of the Grange. From left to right are (first row) Caroline Christiansen Olson, Mrs. R. G. Greene, Maggy Erp, Clarence Worrell, Sibyl Laughlins, Cora May, Mayme Anderson, and Margaret Barr; (second row) Harvey May, Karl Lawrence, Frank Badger, Lottie Kimbel, Adelaide Barr, Harry Meserve, Edward Rice, Edna Spooner, ? Brauger, Lorena Erp, ? Jones, and Chester Laughlin.

A highway fund-raiser for Hungry Highway, the name of the road that was not rocked, took place on August 19, 1928, at Svenson's Corner. Three steamboats, 300 cars, and 3,000 people came to the event. Hungry Highway was only passable during the summertime, and one road in the county is still called by that name. The field at the center is now the Wahkiakum West Telephone Company.

The driver of this horse and buggy in Grays River in 1917 is Margaret Grandberg. In 1927, when Margaret was in high school, she named the school mascots the Naselle Comets.

These five young men set the pace for Naselle-Grays River Valley High School. They were the first basketball team in 1921–1922; from left to right are Eino Pakanen, Charles Keiski, Otto Hill, Victor Ullakko, and Fred Silvola.

The coach of the Knappton Mill basketball team in 1920 was Glenn McAllister. The men who played were men who worked at the mill, and they would play town teams in Naselle, Ilwaco, and Astoria.

This is the Pacific County champion basketball team for 1930–1931. The players and coach are, from left to right, (seated) Reuben Penttila, Charles O'Connor, Harold Wiitala, and coach Dean Lobaugh; (standing) Herb Johnson, Louie Penttila, Clarence Harrison, and Dale Estoos. Naselle has had many outstanding basketball teams over the years since 1931.

The Deep River School boys' baseball team is pictured here in 1915. From left to right are Matt Pouttu, Charles Wirkkala, William Rangila, Otto Bumala, John Lassila, William Bakkila, Ernest Bumala, Ike Pouttu, and Charles Pouttu.

The Deep River baseball team stands on the steps of the Cozy Corner Restaurant in 1912. The team was, from left to right, Alfred Lamppa, Jacob Matta, Henry Johnson, Arvo Davis, manager Fred Mathison, Arthur Anderson, Erick Mathison, unidentified, Peter Matta, Charles Eskola, and batboy Earl Erick.

The Deep River Reds baseball team in 1916 was, from left to right, (first row) Ernest Mathison, Enoch Mathison, unidentified, Charles Eskola, and Henry Johnson; (second row) two unidentified, Frank Potter, and Arvo Davis.

Gary Corcoran, age 18, is pictured on Radar Ridge with his canine in 1955 or 1956 during the air force days in Naselle. Gary was in the Canine Division at the base, a unit they had for two years. The air force base was in Naselle between 1951 and 1966; it was the 759th Aircraft Control and Warning Squadron/Radar Station. Gary now makes his home in Naselle.

Bryant Oman drives his 1949 Ford 8-N tractor in the Eagles Day Parade in Cathlamet, Washington (the county seat of Wahkiakum County). He completely restored it himself at the age of 14. In his hand is the Eagle Trophy he has won for first place in the Farm Machinery Division. Bryant is the great-great-grandson of Chester and Sybil Laughlin, pioneers of Grays River, and the great-grandson of early pioneers to Grays River Hjalmar and Mabyn Klint. The Eagles Day is the third Saturday in July each year.

Visit us at
arcadiapublishing.com

CPSIA information can be obtained
at www.ICGtesting.com
Printed in the USA
BVHW010209261120
594269BV00007B/77

9 781531 637828